We Celebrate
Hallowe'en

Bobbie Kalman

**Allan and Deborah
Drew-Brook-Cormack**

The Holidays & Festivals Series

Crabtree Publishing Company

The Holidays and Festivals Series
Created by Bobbie Kalman

Writing team:
Bobbie Kalman
Susan Hughes

Illustrations:
Allan and Deborah Drew-Brook-Cormack
© Crabtree Publishing Company

Editor-in-chief:
Bobbie Kalman

Editors:
Susan Hughes
Lise Gunby
Grace DeLottinville
Dan Liebman
Jane Lind

Research:
Lise Gunby
Lynne Carson

Cover design:
Peter Maher, Newton Frank Arthur Inc.
Karen Harrison

Art direction and design:
Jane Hamilton
Hugh Michaelson
Catherine Johnston

Mechanicals:
Nancy Cook

For Diane

Cataloguing in Publication Data
Kalman, Bobbie, 1947-
  We celebrate Hallowe'en

(The Holidays and festivals series)
Includes index.
ISBN 0-86505-039-2

1. Hallowe'en. I. Title. II. Series.

GT4965.K35 1985   394.2'683

350 Fifth Avenue   102 Torbrick Avenue
Suite 3308   Toronto, Ontario
New York, N.Y. 10118 Canada M4J 4Z5

Contents

4

Hallowe'en is here again

It's Hallowe'en, the night is dark.
Wild noises fill the air.
The trees have eyes, the sidewalks creak,
The shadows slide and stare.

There is a house that's up our street.
It's old and falling down.
The steps are cracked, the windows sag.
It's the creepiest house in town!

This is the night that we've agreed
To visit the haunted house.
So grit your teeth, hold my hand,
And be quiet as a mouse.

The street is black, the ghosts are out.
We hear their bones clink by.
Witches' brooms just clear our heads,
The imps and pixies fly.

We tiptoe to the haunted house,
A horrible sight to see.
The place seems filled with ghostly guests
Having a ghastly tea.

The windows wink with eerie lights,
The chimney puffs blue smoke.
The purple clouds do somersaults,
The moon laughs at the joke.

With shaking hands and clacking teeth,
We shiver at the door.
The goblins dance, the elves cavort,
The nymphs and fairies soar.

We push our way through thick cobwebs,
And into a corner shrink.
Oh, what a Hallowe'en we'll have.
We'll never sleep a wink!

How Hallowe'en began

Thousands of years ago, there were tribes of people called Celts (pronounced Kelts). The Celts were farmers who lived in many parts of Europe. They knew that the sunshine helped their crops grow. When autumn came, the sunshine began to fade. The Celts believed that the sun would be winter's prisoner for six months.

A fiery festival

The Celts worried that the sun might never return. To make sure it did, they held a festival on October 31. During this festival, they asked the sun to return safely in the summer. All the cooking fires were put out. Then the villagers lit huge bonfires on the hillside. They prayed that the sun would shine brightly after winter was over.

Dressing up

On the morning after the festival, the Celts returned to the hillside. They took pieces of burning wood from the remains of the bonfires. They lit new fires with these. They believed that the new fires would bring good luck. Huge feasts were cooked over the new fires. Everyone dressed in costumes made of animal skins. It was believed that these costumes would protect the people from bad luck.

This is how Hallowe'en began. Ever since the festival celebrated by the Celts, people have been dressing up in costumes on Hallowe'en.

Tonight's the night!

"It's Hallowe'en, it's Hallowe'en," howled James. James was practicing his werewolf walk. He jumped around the room. He scared the cat which then leaped across his mother's back. "Hurry up and get dressed," James called to his brothers and sisters. "It's Hallowe'en, it's Hallowe'en. Ahwoooo."

9

"What's a snuffle?"

"Please, James," Laurel said in a grown-up voice. "We're trying to get ready for trick-or-treating."

"Ahwooo!" James answered, making a growling face at his sister. "Ahwooo do you think you are?"

Laurel stuck out her tongue between her lipsticked lips. "A fancy lady," she answered. James laughed because Laurel had lipstick on her nose!

"Candy, candy, candy," said James. "Ahwooo!" James yanked Paul's long donkey ears. "What's your favorite candy, donkey?" he asked.

Paul smiled. "Chocolate bars!" he cried. Then he frowned. "Do you think people will give candy to a donkey? I hate carrots!"

Charlie's big mouse ears twitched. "Squeak!" he squealed. "Will they give me cheese? No cheese please! I want candy apples."

Laurel began to list her favorite Hallowe'en treats. "I like gumdrops, candy kisses, and caramel corn. Oh, and fudge, chocolate bars, and potato chips.

And then there's peanuts, licorice shoelaces, jelly beans, mints. . .''

''Laurel,'' Sam interrupted. ''Maybe you should just tell us what Hallowe'en treats you *don't* like!''

Sam was grumpy because he could not think of a good costume to wear.

''Maybe you could be a witch with a crooked nose,'' Laurel said to Sam.

''Or a ghost with no eyes,'' shivered James.

''Or a skeleton in chains,'' said Charlie.

''Nah,'' said Sam. He thought for a moment. ''I will be a Snuffle.''

His brothers and sisters looked at him. They looked at one another. They looked at their father. They looked at Sam again. ''A what?'' they asked.

Sam winked. ''A Snuffle with a green tail,'' he said. ''It's Hallowe'en, remember? Anything is possible on Hallowe'en!''

Make your own costumes

The Celts dressed up in animal skins on October 31. Now *we* dress up in costumes on Hallowe'en. Make your own costumes using things found around your home. Dress up as a witch, a ghost, or a goblin. You can be a big butterfly with brightly-colored paper wings. Be a growing plant. Wear something green and slowly raise your arms. You can be Superman or Superwoman, but do not try to fly! Be topsy-turvy by wearing your clothes inside out.

Wrap around

Think of all the costumes you can make with a sheet. Cut out two eyes and you are a ghost. Wrap the sheet around you and you are an ancient Roman wearing a toga. Cut the sheet into strips. Wrap them around you. Now you have been transformed into an Egyptian mummy.

Garbage-bag fun

What can you make with a green garbage bag? Cut holes for your legs and step inside. Fill in the bag with old newspapers. Cut holes for your arms. Gather the top of the bag loosely at your neck and fasten it with a red ribbon. Wear a red hat. You are now an olive stuffed with pimento. Wear a green garbage bag, green stockings, and a green cap with a feather in it. Hello, Robin Hood! Blow up some green or purple balloons and attach them to the bag with some strong tape. You are now a bunch of grapes! Be careful **never** to put the unopened end of a bag over your head. Ask an older person to help you with these costume ideas.

Get inside a box

Find a large box. Add knobs and dials. Step inside the box and you are a talking computer or a robot. You can add a pointed top to the box and become a spaceship. Decorate the box with a picture. You are now a television set. Carry a spoon and be a cereal box. Wear a long tall box and be a package of spaghetti. It is important to be sure that your costume leaves your line of vision clear when you are walking outside.

Use your imagination

Be an animal, a vegetable, or a character from your favorite story or movie. Be a sports star or a magician. Be someone who lived a long time ago or someone who might live in the future. Be a rag doll, a video game, a bumblebee, or a tiger. Be anything you want to be. Use your imagination!

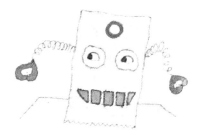

Trick-or-treat?

People are not sure how trick-or-treating began. There are many stories to explain this custom. This story describes one way that trick-or-treating might have begun.

Fooling the spirits

Long ago, many people believed that ghosts walked on Hallowe'en. They believed that fairies and ghouls played tricks on human beings. What did people do to fool the spirits? They put on costumes.

14

One Hallowe'en, a long time ago, a group of young people called on a neighbor. When the neighbor poked her head out the door, she gave a gasp of alarm. She did not realize that these "creatures" at the door were young people from the village who had put on costumes. She thought that they were spirits who had come to play tricks on her. How could she prevent them from playing pranks?

She had an idea. She ran to her kitchen and came back a minute later. She gave the "spirits" food and money so that they would leave. The visitors were surprised by the treats. They thanked their neighbor kindly and went on to the next house. The same thing happened! Soon these young people had visited every house in the village. They had so much fun, they decided they would go visiting in their costumes every Hallowe'en!

Trick-or-treat rhymes
Some people think that this tradition led to asking for treats on Hallowe'en. How do you ask for treats?

Do you say: Shell out, shell out,
           The witches are out!

or:
Trick-or-treat, you're so neat.
I know you'll give us lots of treats.
Some nuts and candy, fruit and gum.
We'll go away after you give us some.

or:
Trick-or-treat, smell my feet.
Give me something good to eat.
Not too big, not too small,
Just the size of Montreal.

What's in a name?
Many people believed that on October 31 and November 1, the souls of the dead came back to earth to visit their families and friends. People began to call the first day of November a holy or "hallowed" day. It became known as All Hallow's Day. The night of October 31 was called All Hallow's Evening. Can you see how this name was shortened to become Hallowe'en?

Soul-caking
Everyone wanted to welcome the friendly spirits. Villagers in Great Britain baked special soul-cakes for them. When children dressed up in costumes and called at their neighbors' homes on All Hallow's Eve, their neighbors gave them soul-cakes, too!

"That tree is alive!"

The parade of trick-or-treaters is marching
bravely through the moonlit night.

''Quack,'' says Sally, who is a duck.

''Hee-haw,'' answers Paul, who is a donkey.

Sam shakes his head at Sally and Paul.
''Listen, you two,'' he says. ''Hallowe'en is
not just a night for pretending. You think
Hallowe'en is funny. But you'll see.
Hallowe'en is scary. Crazy things happen.
Ghosts are real.''

''Boo!'' shouts Laurel.

16

Everyone jumps. Sam jumps the highest of all. Laurel giggles.

Suddenly, all the children squeak, howl, quack, and honk. The gigantic oak tree is snarling! It shakes its leafy hair. Its fingers are knotty, and they grab at the children. The tree begins to moan: "Beware. Beware."

The children dash away. They do not want to hear the rest of the message.

The scariest house in town

The children skid to a stop at the first house they see. They are afraid to turn around. Are they safe now? They bang the door-knocker loudly. No one answers the door. The children hold their breath. Clara looks at the door. The knocker looks like a snake. Clara squirms.

Paul steps back to look at the huge house. There is a gigantic orange pumpkin scowling from the window. ''Hee-haw,'' brays Paul, in his donkey costume.

A black cat with golden eyes rubs against Charlie's leg. ''Squeak,'' cries Charlie, the mouse. Laurel shouts at the cat: ''Boo!'' But the cat does not blink an eye. James peeks through the front window. Everything is dark inside. ''Ahwoooo,'' howls James, the werewolf. ''Listen,'' quacks Sally, the duck. ''I hear footsteps.''

The door grinds open, slowly. The children squint through the empty doorway. ''Hello?'' Sam snuffles. ''Is anybody home?''

A tall twisted shape crashes down in front of them. Is it a witch? Is it a ghost? Its eyes bulge. It has bright orange hair that sticks straight out from its head. It speaks! ''Aren't you going to say trick-or-treat? It is Hallowe'en, you know,'' it says.

James topples back. He trips on Charlie's long mouse tail. Charlie grabs at Paul's drooping donkey ears as he falls. Paul slips on Sally's floppy duck feet. Sally slides on Laurel's big bouncing skirt. Laurel clutches at Clara. Clara's mask slides over her eyes and she falls down.

The creature cackles.

''Trrrickkk-or-trrreattt?'' quaver the children, all in a pile at the front door.

''Trick!'' giggles the creature as it swirls its orange hair. ''Trick!''

The children scramble up and race away. They do not want to play a trick on this ghoulish character. They never want to see this weird monster again!

The night's adventures have only just begun. Can you imagine other adventures that the children might have on this Hallowe'en?

19

Collect for UNICEF

Hallowe'en is a night of ghosts, jack-o'-lanterns, and costumes. It is a night for collecting treats. Hallowe'en is also a night to help others. Do you know how you can help other children on Hallowe'en? Sometimes you are given coins when you go trick-or-treating. Collect all your coins and take them to school. Your teacher can help you find a good cause to which you can donate your coins.

You can also collect coins in a UNICEF box. UNICEF stands for United Nations International Children's Emergency Fund. When UNICEF receives your coins, it puts them with the coins that other children have collected. Then UNICEF uses the money to buy food and medicine for children around the world. Collecting for UNICEF is a way to share your Hallowe'en with children who are not as fortunate as you are.

Are you superstitious?

Do you believe in bad luck? Do you believe in ghosts and goblins? Of course not! But once a year, it's fun to let our imaginations run wild. It's fun to tell ghost stories and shiver at a pumpkin's stare. Even Adam thinks so!

Adam's Hallowe'en

Adam is like you and me-
He doesn't believe in ghosts.
Adam's not superstitious
And of this he likes to boast.

Adam's favorite number
Has always been thirteen,
And if it falls on Friday
He is always just as keen.

Adam goes under ladders.
He lets black cats cross his way.
He doesn't believe in bad luck.
''There's no such thing,'' he'll say.

Adam sees a bright star.
It falls down with a swish.
But he's not superstitious,
So he doesn't make a wish.

22

Adam walks the sidewalk
And he steps on every crack.
He knows this simple action
Won't break his mother's back.

Adam's favorite dinner
Is a turkey big and stout,
But Adam won't make wishes,
So he throws the wishbone out.

The last day of October
Means Hallowe'en is here.
Adam is excited.
It's the best day of the year.

Adam goes trick-or-treating.
He thinks Hallowe'en is fun.
He pretends that he is frightened.
If he saw a ghost, he'd run.

He won't walk under ladders,
He hides from a cat that's black,
He wishes on stars and wishbones,
And he won't step on a crack.

Though he's not superstitious
And he knows there are no ghosts,
Adam likes Hallowe'en
And of this he often boasts.

FRIDAY THE 13TH!

WISH I MAY, WISH I MIGHT

23

A night of enchantment

A night of enchantment

It's Hallowe'en night and the moon is aglow.
My parents are sleeping. It's time now to go!

I creep out of bed and I run through the dark.
I see the trees shake and hear the dogs bark.

Through the woods to the glade, I run with the breeze;
Branches tickle my nose but I try not to sneeze.

The fairies come flying in a circle of light.
The goblins are dancing on this Hallowe'en night.

The elves play the music, the witches look on.
The party will last from midnight 'til dawn.

I watch as the spirits sing songs and weave spells.
They flit over flowers, they jingle like bells.

The night is alive with the sounds of their glee.
They love Hallowe'en — it's their night to be free!

I watch and I watch 'til the first light of day.
Then the pixies and elves scurry sadly away.

Shuffling their feet, all the goblins and trolls
Disappear into magical tunnels and holes.

The witches and fairies slip into the sky
And they twirl their way home on the breath of a sigh.

I rub my eyes once and my yawns greet the sun.
The Hallowe'en night of enchantment is done.

26

Strange things happen on Hallowe'en

Have you ever seen a witch, a goblin, a fairy, an elf, a troll, or a gnome? Not many people have! But some people believe that Hallowe'en is the best night of the year to try to see these magical beings. Hallowe'en is their favorite celebration. Fairies come out of their homes hidden inside the hills. They dance and frolic by the light of the moon. Elves prance out of their caves in the rocks. Goblins stomp through villages, peering into dark corners. Pixies meet in the meadows to skip in a sparkling circle. Witches dart and swoop through the moonlit sky.

The "little people" play big pranks

People tell strange stories about things that happen on Hallowe'en. Fresh milk turns sour. Gates are opened, and wagons are found on the roofs of barns. Soap is smeared on windows, and rocking chairs are found swaying in treetops. Who is responsible for these practical jokes? On Hallowe'en, the "little people" are usually to blame.

Watch out for elves and fairies

In one English village, it was told that some elves rode on the backs of the villagers' cats. The cats had fun but the villagers were very frightened. Every Hallowe'en after that, the village folks locked their cats up so that the elves could not catch them.

Children were told not to sit in the circles of yellow or white flowers that grew in the meadows. The circles of flowers grew where fairy feet danced. If a child sat in the Fairy Ring, he or she might be stolen by the fairies. It was also believed dangerous to sit under the hawthorn tree on Hallowe'en. The hawthorn is a thorny shrub or small tree. The fairies loved to dance on the hawthorn. It did not seem to prickle their toes. But if they saw a child sitting under it, their tempers were prickled.

Selena's special day

It was October 30, the night before Hallowe'en. Selena went to bed early because she knew she would be up late at Billy's Hallowe'en party the next night. Selena wasn't tired. She tossed and turned. Finally, she fell into a restless sleep and began to dream. Selena dreamt that on Hallowe'en, she became a witch and had magical powers for the day.

In her dream, Selena went to Billy's party. All the children were dressed up in colorful costumes. Stephen was dressed as a pumpkin. Susan was a black cat. Adelaide was an elf. Can you guess what Selena's costume was?

You are right! Selena was dressed as a witch. When Stephen saw Selena, he laughed and said, ''You look just like a real witch, Selena. Really ugly!'' Selena laughed too. She was ready to play her first trick. She pointed her broomstick at Stephen. She made a wish. BOINGG!

Topsy-turvy fun

Stephen's pumpkin eyes blinked. Then he said, "Apples for bob let's."
Selena laughed. She could understand Stephen but no one else could.
Susan stared at Stephen. "Why are you talking strangely?" she asked him.

Stephen looked at Susan as if she was the one who was acting funny. He
did not know that his words were backwards. "Bob let's," he said again
and walked with the other children to the tub filled with apples.

As Selena watched Susan bobbing for apples, she had an idea for another
trick. When Susan lifted her cat face and her wet whiskers from the tub,
she had a big red apple in her mouth. Selena winked and snapped her
fingers. BOINGG!

Susan took the apple out of her mouth and said, "My face is all wet. I look
funny, I bet. What prize do I get?" "Susan, that rhymed!" laughed Billy.
"Don't be silly. You're teasing me, Billy," Susan said. She did not know
that she was under a spell.

Everyone laughed. Selena laughed the loudest of all. She liked to see her
friends enjoying her tricks. Selena did not want Adelaide to feel left out.
BOINGG! Adelaide's elf ears twitched. Adelaide smiled happily as she
said, "I hate Hallowe'en. This has been a terrible party."

Billy heard Adelaide and was surprised. "I thought you had a good time,"
he said to her. Adelaide gave Billy a strange look. "That's what I just said.
This has been a terrible party," she repeated. "I hope you don't have
another one next year." She smiled at him.

Selena laughed at the surprised look on Billy's face. "Adelaide is playing a
Hallowe'en trick," Billy decided with a grin. "Hallowe'en makes people
very silly. I'm glad she thought my party was so much fun."

It was time to go home. "Watch out for witches on your way home," Billy
called, as Adelaide, Susan, Stephen, and Selena waved good-bye.

Many crazy things happened as Selena and her friends walked home.
Doorbells sounded like car horns, dogs meowed, cats walked backwards,
flowers bloomed in the dark, and lights flickered. Who do you think was
making these things happen?

Just before Stephen said good-bye to Selena, he turned to her and said, "Wouldn't it be fun if there were real witches?" "But there are witches, Stephen," Selena said. Stephen laughed. "Silly Selena," he said. "You are a nut if you really believe in witches." Selena smiled and thought to herself, "Next year I just might turn Stephen into a huge, green frog!"

Suddenly, Selena woke up with a picture of a frog in her mind. "What on earth was I dreaming about?" Selena asked her cat. "It must have been a Hallowe'en nightmare!"

Cat magic

Why do we think of cats when we think of Hallowe'en? Cats have always been special animals. The Celts believed that spirits could look like cats. They believed that cats could predict the future.

Black cats have always been a part of people's superstitions. Superstitions are beliefs that something bad may happen because something else takes place. In North America, Ireland, Belgium, and Spain, some people still believe that it is bad luck to let a black cat cross their paths. Some people say that it is unlucky for a black cat to come into their homes or travel on their ships. But a white cat is different. It is supposed to bring good luck. In England, however, it is the opposite. People believe that black cats are lucky and white cats unlucky. In Russia, cats that bring luck are blue. Have you ever seen a blue cat?

My sweet black cat

I have a black cat.
She's shy and she's sweet.
But on Hallowe'en night
When she walks down the street,

Everyone runs
To get out of her way.
She doesn't know why:
She's more frightened than they!

Hallowe'en spells

In her dream, Selena put spells on her friends. Her spells were silent. She just pointed her broom or snapped her fingers. Here are some Hallowe'en spells. Which one of these would you like to hear Selena say to you? Try making up some funny spells at your Hallowe'en party.

Wings of bats and chicken gizzards,
Eyes of snakes and tails of lizards,
Navels of apes and a witch's sneeze.
May the corns on your toes reach to your
knees.

Pumpkin seeds and carrot tops,
Bones of skeletons and warlocks' mops,
Ghastly howls and the screams of a troll.
May you find a goblin in your cereal bowl.

Teeth of crocodiles and knees of goats,
Tongues of frogs and warts of toads,
Elbows of flies and a werewolf's fang.
May bats upside down from your armpits
hang.

Tops of toadstools and poison oak,
Goblins' slippers and Dracula's cloak,
A black cat's fur and roast of mutton.
May tulips sprout from your bellybutton.

Mosquito stingers and those of bees,
The nips and bites of a thousand fleas,
Ears of lambs and a buffalo's nose.
May an army of red ants invade your toes.

Zebra stripes and leopard spots,
Rattlesnakes all tied up in knots.
May spinach, turnip, and a lima bean
Be all you get on Hallowe'en!

Hallowe'en words

Try to use all these words in your own Hallowe'en story.

witch

ghost, ghoul, spirit

broom

fairy, elf, pixie, imp, nymph

mask

skeleton

costume

goblin, gremlin, gnome, troll

bonfire

34

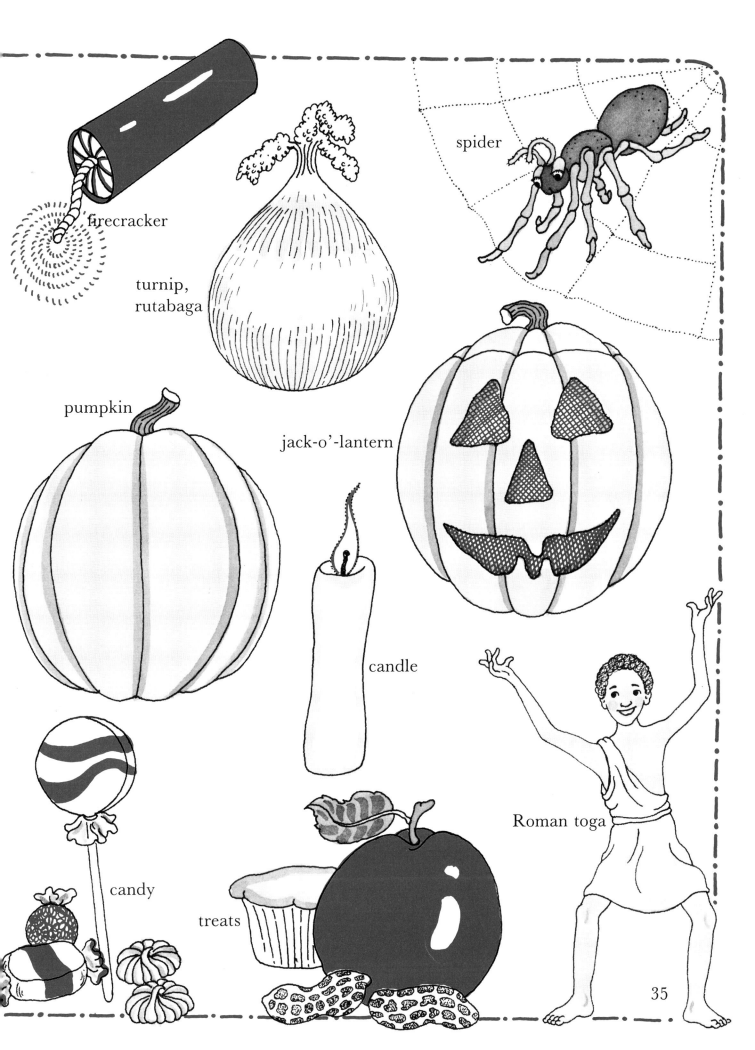

firecracker

turnip,
rutabaga

spider

pumpkin

jack-o'-lantern

candle

Roman toga

candy

treats

35

Punkie fun

On Hallowe'en, children in Ireland and Scotland cut scary faces into hollowed-out turnips, large rutabagas, or potatoes. They put candles inside. In England, children make ''punkies'' out of large beets. They cut a window, a face, or a beautiful design into the beets. Then they carry the punkies through the streets and sing the Punkie Night Song. They knock on doors and ask for money.

In some parts of England, turnip lanterns are placed on gateposts to protect homes from the spirits who play tricks. In the United States and Canada, many people welcome trick-or-treaters by placing lighted pumpkins called jack-o'-lanterns in their windows.

Making a jack-o'-lantern

Choose the biggest pumpkin you can find. Cut off its top. Dig in with your fingers and pull out the mushy pulp. Draw the scariest face you can think of on the pumpkin. Ask an adult to help you carve the face into the pumpkin. Stick a candle inside. Your pumpkin is now a jack-o'-lantern.

Tricky Jack

An Irish folktale tells us where the name jack-o'-lantern came from. A long time ago, a man named Jack played many tricks on people. He lived a long, mischievous life.

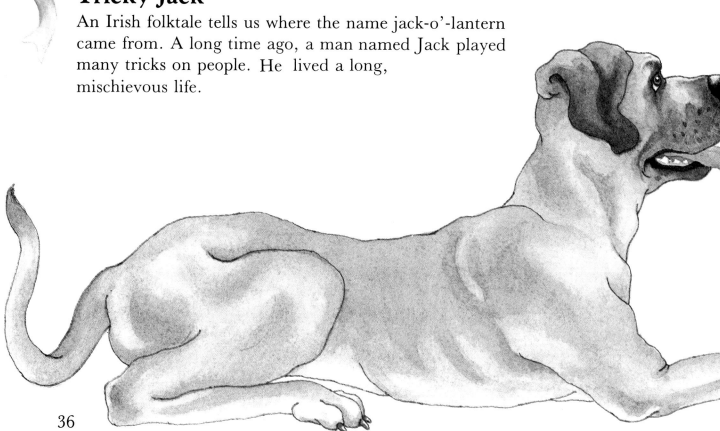

When he died, Jack was sent on an endless journey as a punishment for being too tricky. He carried a burning coal inside a turnip to help him see along the dark roads. Jack had his turnip lantern with him everywhere he traveled. Soon he was known as "Jack of the lantern" or Jack-o'-lantern.

Party Preparations

Why not have a Hallowe'en party this year? Begin to plan your party a week or two before the party date. On construction paper, sketch witches on broomsticks, scowling jack-o'-lanterns, black cats, or blinking owls. Write invitations on the reverse side of your sketches. Make up a funny verse or a spooky poem such as this one:

Come to our Hallowe'en party
With the other ghouls and ghosts.
There is a "boo"by prize
For the best costumes — signed, Your Hosts.

Decorations for your party

Make the party room a fun place to be. Remember that Hallowe'en comes at a time of year when fruits and vegetables are being harvested. Set apples, nuts, and grapes in bowls around the room. Turn pumpkins into jack-o'-lanterns. You can also make jack-o'-lanterns from oranges. Slice off the top of an orange. Scoop out the pulp. The orange skin will harden. Paint scary faces on these miniature lanterns. Fill them with candy.

Hang balloons from the ceiling. Be sure to use orange and yellow balloons, because these are Hallowe'en colors. Hang colored crepe-paper streamers from the corners of the room.

Flying ghosts

Make flying ghosts. Draw ghost shapes on white construction paper. Use crayons to decorate the ghosts. You can give your ghosts freckles or big noses, glasses or red cheeks. Cut strips of construction paper for hair and glue them to the ghosts. Make many ghosts. Hang a thread from one wall to another. Staple each ghost to the thread. Your ghosts will float in the air all night!

Make a Hallowe'en mobile

Find a small fallen branch. You can hang the branch from the ceiling with a piece of wool or a thin wire. On a piece of construction paper, paint a witch stirring a bubbling pot. Paint a grinning jack-o'-lantern and a hooting owl on other pieces of construction paper. Cut out the figures and use thread to hang them from the branch.

Tissue ghosts

You can add a ghost to your mobile. Crumple a piece of tissue paper into a ball. This will form the ghost's head. Then put another piece of tissue paper over the crumpled ball. Use a thread to tie the ball inside the second piece of tissue paper. The outside tissue should hang down from the head as a sheet would hang over a person. Paint two eyes (or three!) on the head.

Thread a needle. Knot the thread. Push the needle into the bottom of the ghost head and out of the top. Cut off the needle. Tie the ghost to the mobile. Let it dangle with the other ghoulish creatures.

Taste the witches' brew

Leg of toad and eye of newt,
A shriveled worm and a smelly boot,
Three dead minnows and a werewolf's tail,
Six mushroom stems and a rusty nail.

Into the pot and then add more:
An aardvark's nose and a giant's snore,
Eight spiders' toes and a wizard's hat,
Five skeleton bones and the tail of a bat.

Stir it all up and stir once again.
Add whiskers of fish and elbows of hen,
Six bellies of leech and eight slimy slugs.
Add two warts of toad and twenty bedbugs.

The pot starts to boil. Come one, come all!
Fly in on brooms or on backs of snails crawl.
This is the witches' Hallowe'en brew.
Come those who dare — have a sip or two!

Disgustingly delicious!

Witches serve some pretty horrible brews at their Hallowe'en parties. You can make your friends think you are serving terrible treats at your party. The following recipes sound bad and look terrible, but don't let that fool you. They taste delicious! If you are planning to try them, make sure you ask someone to help you. Do not use the stove on your own.

Swamp-water Punch

1 large can concentrated
   orange juice
same amount water
1 L (about 1 quart) white grape juice
5 drops green food coloring
washed, assorted plastic spiders,
   flies in plastic ice cubes, rubber
   snakes, or other gory plastic crawlies
1 large bottle carbonated lemon-lime
   soda pop

1. Put everything except plastic crawlies and soda into a large punch bowl and stir.
2. Dump 2 trays of ice cubes into bowl.
3. Float washed plastic crawlies on top of punch.
4. When your friends are ready for a drink, pour the soda into the bowl. The concoction will start to fizz and bubble, bouncing your flies, spiders, and snakes in and out of the ghastly brew!

Sweet and Sour Mud Dip

125 mL (1/2 cup) grape jelly
125 mL (1/2 cup) ketchup
12 cooked hotdogs
toothpicks

1. Put grape jelly into a saucepan.
2. Set saucepan on stove on medium heat.
3. Stir until jelly dissolves.
4. Blend in ketchup.
5. Taste. The mixture should have a sweet and sour taste. If it is too sweet, add more ketchup; if too sour, add more jelly.
6. Cut cooked hotdogs into bite-size pieces and put a toothpick into each piece.

Serve hotdogs with Mud Dip.

Goblin Crunch Cookies

500 mL (2 cups) flour
125 mL (1/2 cup) sugar
250 mL (1 cup) crushed potato chips
250 mL (1 cup) very soft butter
125 mL (1/2 cup) chopped nuts
   (walnuts, almonds, or hazelnuts)

1. Crush potato chips; roll a rolling pin over unopened chip bag or crunch chips with your clean hands.
2. Mix all ingredients together using your hands. Make sure butter moistens all dry ingredients. Squish mixture between fingers. Feels yucky!
3. Roll mixture into little balls and place well apart on ungreased cookie sheets. Flatten balls with a fork.
4. Bake cookies in preheated oven at 180°C (350°F) about 10 minutes or until they are light brown.

Dracula Dip

500 mL (2 cups) sour cream
1 envelope dry tomato-vegetable
   soup mix

1. Put dry soup and sour cream into a bowl.
2. Stir until soup mix is moist.
3. Put mixture into refrigerator for at least 2 hours.

Serve with chips or raw vegetables.

Rocky Horrors

500 mL (2 cups) semi-sweet
   chocolate chips
500 mL (2 cups) peanuts
375 mL (1 1/2 cups) sweetened
   condensed milk
30 mL (2 tablespoons) butter
10 mL (2 teaspoons) vanilla
280 g (10 ounces) miniature
   marshmallows

1. Put chips, condensed milk, and butter into saucepan.
2. Set saucepan on low heat.
3. Stir mixture as it melts.
4. When melted, remove from stove and stir in vanilla and nuts.
5. Let mixture cool.
6. Place marshmallows in a large bowl and stir in chocolate mixture.
7. Line a 23 cm by 33 cm (9'' x 13'') pan with waxed paper.
8. Spread mixture evenly in pan.
9. Chill about 2 hours or until firm.
10. Remove from pan and peel off waxed paper.
11. Cut into squares.

Have a howling Hallowe'en party

Make the "disgustingly delicious" treats before the party. Send out invitations and ask your friends to dress in costumes. Decorate the party room. Prepare ghoulish games.

Will your party be as much fun as this one? These children are playing Blindman's Buff. This game has been played on Hallowe'en for many years. The robot with the blindfold must catch one of the guests. Then, without taking off his blindfold, he must try to guess that person's identity. That is hard to do even with his eyes open. Everyone is wearing good disguises!

Apples for Pomona

Why are apple games so popular at Hallowe'en? Apples ripen in the autumn. Hallowe'en is also in autumn. Thousands of years ago, during the time of the early Romans, autumn was a very special season. On October 31 each year, the Romans had a huge celebration to honor Pomona, the goddess of fruit. They thanked Pomona for the harvest. People played games and ran races. They enjoyed a big feast. They offered up apples and nuts to Pomona. Ever since those days, apples have been a big part of Hallowe'en.

Apple games

Start your party with some Hallowe'en apple games.

1. Tie an apple to a string hanging from a doorway or ceiling. Hold your hands behind your back and try to bite the swinging fruit.
2. Two players kneel on newspapers with a chair between them. Two apples are placed on the chair. The players' hands are held behind their backs. On the word "Go!" the players must race to see who can finish eating an apple first. If the apple falls to the ground, the player is out of the game.

A seedy game

Counting the Seeds is a game that many children can play. Give each guest an apple that has been cut in half. Each person counts the number of seeds in his or her piece. People used to believe that the number of seeds in an apple could reveal something about a person's future. Two seeds in the apple meant an early marriage; three, an inheritance; four, great wealth; five, a trip across the ocean; and six, fame. Seven seeds meant that the person's wishes would come true. How many seeds did you find in your apple?

Paring up

Another apple game is the Initial Letter game. Pare a green apple in one long, winding piece. Swing the paring over your head three times, singing:

Paring, paring, long and green,
Tell my fate for Hallowe'en.

Drop the paring behind you. When a paring forms the shape of a letter, that letter is believed to be the first initial of the person you will marry.

Apple bobbing

Apple bobbing is a favorite Hallowe'en game. It has been played for hundreds of years. Why don't you try it? Fill a large tub or pail with water. Drop in several apples. They will float on the surface of the water. Now comes the fun part. Kneel or stand by the side of the tub with your hands behind your back. Choose the apple that looks the biggest and juiciest. Take a deep breath and open your mouth wide. Now comes the bobbing. Can you grab the apple with your teeth?

49

Hallowe'en games

Cat Conversation

Sit in a circle and play some games. Have a Cat Conversation. Each guest must say a sentence that includes a word containing "cat" as a syllable. The leader may begin by talking about the "new *cat*alog." The next player may say, "I didn't *cat*ch what you said," or "I like *cat*sup." If a player is not quick enough to say his or her sentence, the group shouts, "*S*cat!" The player must leave the circle. The last remaining player is the winner.

Ghost Messages

Try sending Ghost Messages. Set a bowl of lemon juice on the table. Give each guest a toothpick and a piece of paper. Tell the guests to dip their toothpicks into the lemon juice and then write a message on the paper. Let the juice dry and exchange papers. How can the messages be read? Hold the paper in front of a warm light bulb. The letters will darken. Now read the secret Ghost Messages.

That's a laugh

Have some fun making up Hallowe'en jokes. These will give you a start:

Q: Why did the witches go on strike?
A: They wanted electric brooms.

Q: What do you call a pumpkin with a burned-out candle?
A: A jack-o'-blackout.

Q: Where do bats get their energy?
A: From their bat-trees.

Q: Where did the little bat have to go?
A: To the bat-room.

A ghastly game

Sit in a circle. Ask your guests to close their eyes, or give them blindfolds. Pass these objects as they are called for in the story: dried apricots; skinned grapes; cold, long pieces of carrot; corn silk or cooked spinach; cooked rice; cooked wet spaghetti; kernels of dry corn; banana, cut in half, then cut lengthwise.

50

Monster mush

Now begin your story like this:

There was a monster who lived in a rotting, crumbling, haunted house. He ate frogs for dinner. One Hallowe'en, he was out at a monster party. On his way home, he was crossing a swamp when a huge storm came up. The monster drowned. Since then, parts of the monster's body have floated on top of the swamp each eerie Hallowe'en. We are going to pass them to you!

This huge monster once could hear.
Now he no longer has an ear.
(Pass apricots.)

All the frogs had a surprise
When they bobbed past the
   monster's eyes.
(Pass grapes.)

None of the frogs dared to linger
When they saw the monster's
   floating finger.
(Pass carrot.)

Through the swamp without a care
Drifted the monster's slimy hair.
(Pass corn silk or spinach.)

When the monster took his swim
All these maggots jumped from him.
(Pass rice.)

The swamp was filled with the
   monster's veins.
They rise to the surface when it rains.
(Pass spaghetti.)

The frog-eating monster never smiled
Until he had his teeth all filed.
(Pass corn kernels.)

When into the swamp the monster
   was flung,
His teeth clamped down and he bit
   off his tongue.
(Pass banana.)

All Souls' Day

Many people around the world have parties and celebrations in late October or early November. Hallowe'en or All Hallow's Eve is October 31. November 1 is All Hallow's Day or All Saints' Day. November 2 is All Souls' Day. People believe that on these days, the spirits of the dead return to visit their graves and their families. People want to welcome these spirits with beauty, warmth, and food.

In many countries, families visit cemeteries together. They decorate the graves with bundles of flowers and wreaths. In Portugal, people have feasts of wine and chestnuts at the cemetery. Mexicans have picnic lunches on the graves of their relatives. This is a day of remembrance, happiness, and celebration.

Beans and bones

The Mexicans bake bread and make candy in the shape of a skull and crossbones, a casket, or a skeleton. Italians make cakes in the shape of beans. These cakes are called ''Beans of the Dead.'' The Portuguese bake special sugar cakes flavored with cinnamon and herbs. In Spain, a special pastry, called ''Bones of the Holy,'' is eaten on this day.

Songs and treats

In most of these countries, children go from door to door singing rhymes or traditional songs which celebrate the spirits of the dead. The children are treated to the special breads or cakes. Mexican children run through the streets with lanterns and ask for coins. Does this remind you of the children who went soul-caking many years ago in Britain? Does this remind you of trick-or-treating?

Lighting the way

In Belgium, Italy, and the Philippines, people light candles in the memory of their dead relatives. In Italy and Austria, people leave bread, water, and a lighted lamp on the table when they go to bed. This is to welcome the dead souls. In Mexico, people light bonfires and set off firecrackers. They hang lanterns on trees to guide home the dead souls. In Poland, the doors and windows are left open to welcome the visiting souls. In Czechoslovakia, chairs are drawn up to the fireside. There is a chair for each family member and one for each family spirit. People in Germany put their knives away. They do not want to risk hurting the returning spirits.

O-Bon

The Japanese O-Bon festival also celebrates the memory of dead relatives. Food and water are placed in front of photographs of the dead. Bonfires and lanterns light the spirits' paths back to earth. China has a similar festival called Teng Chieh.

The Hungry Ghosts Festival

In Hong Kong, there is a festival similar to Hallowe'en. During the Hungry Ghosts Festival or Yue Lan, ghosts and spirits roam the world for 24 hours. Some people burn pictures of fruit or money. They believe that when these presents are burned, they reach the spirit world and comfort the ghosts on this day.

Customs and traditions similar to Hallowe'en occur all over the world. People everywhere share many of the same beliefs.

Good-bye ghosts, ghouls, goblins, and gremlins

The sun has chased the night away.
Now Hallowe'en has passed.
Our visit to the haunted house
Is finished all too fast.

This crooked house has rocked all night
With the party of the ghouls.
They invented games, they laughed,
   they sang.
They shattered all the rules.

We sat and watched the gremlins dance,
We heard the goblins shout.
The ghouls and ghosts played
   hide-and-seek,
The house turned inside out.

They flew too high, they flew too low,
They made these old walls shake.
They danced above, they danced below,
They never took a break!

But now the ghosts must travel home
Wherever that may be!
Hallowe'en is gone for another year
For the ghouls, my friends, and me.

And as we watch them fade away,
We all smile at the sight.
For we'll be back at the haunted house
Next year, on Hallowe'en night.

Index

456789 BP Printed in Canada 432109

56